I0004930

How to
Change the World
In 30 Seconds

A Web Warrior's Guide
to Animal Advocacy Online
2013 Edition

C.A.Wulff

Barking Planet Productions

Marblehead, Massachusetts

How to Change the World in 30 Seconds:
A Web Warrior's Guide to Animal Advocacy Online
Copyright © 2013
by Cayr Ariel Wulff and Dalene E. Dilworth.
All rights reserved.
First Edition

ISBN
0-9786928-8-8
978-09786928-8-9

Library of Congress Control Number: 2013901324

Publisher: Barking Planet Productions
Marblehead, Massachusetts

Photo credits: Cover photo: 1st Gallery – Fotolia.com
Page 5: Chris Hughes, Page 27: Krysta Mullins,
Page 28: Deborah Eades, Page 29: Misty Riley,
Page 40: Kathleen Varga, Page 54: Nancy Tullis,
Page 59: Rosemarie La Pierre, Page 67: Pamela Kramer

Dedicated to all of the individuals and groups who devote their heads, hands, and hearts to improving the world for companion animals. You are all, every one of you, my heroes.

Author's Note:

Because the Internet is constantly changing, I cannot guarantee that the websites listed in this book will be active indefinitely. My hope is to update this guide as changes and growth warrant.

If you are part of a rescue group and would like to use copies of this guide for fundraising, please contact me on my Facebook author page: C.A.Wulff
[https://www.facebook.com/pages/CAWulff/15689 8504349943?ref=ts&fref=ts]

Table of Contents

Acknowledgements

Grateful thanks for the support from early readers Bob Tarte, Deborah Eades, Scott Heiser, Tamira Ci Thayne, John Woestendiek, and Kathy Smola, who answered my frantic cries for help and graciously allowed me to impinge upon their time and projects. Thanks also to Rosemarie LaPierre, Pamela Kramer, Chris Hughes and Kathleen Varga who shared stories of their rescue dogs with me. Finally, my deepest gratitude to Bob & Stella McCarty at Barking Planet Productions for their generous support and unwavering belief in my work.

Introduction

I SAVED A LIFE TODAY. It was one of several dozen lives that I have saved this year, and each time, it took me only 30 seconds. But that's not all -- this year I also prevented the torture of hundreds of innocents, and prevented the illness of thousands more. I am not a super hero, a doctor or a member of the military; I am an animal advocate.

Indian philosopher and social activist Mahatma Gandhi said *"The greatness of a nation and its moral progress can be judged by the way its animals are treated."*

The truth of that statement is made evident by the fact that more progressive countries have laws related to animal welfare, and less progressive countries around the globe do not. In the United States alone, the way companion animals are treated today is vastly different from how they were treated fifty years ago. The number of Americans with the desire to save and improve the lives of companion animals has increased dramatically and continues to grow as more people become educated about animal welfare issues.

Although you may want to help animals, you may not have any idea where to begin. Or maybe you think that you don't have enough time to make a difference. This guide will offer practical steps to get started using dog advocacy as the focus and will explain how just thirty seconds a day on the Internet can not only make a difference, but can also *change the world*.

Chapter <u>One</u>
Changing the World

T HERE'S A SAYING HEARD repeatedly in animal advocacy and rescue:

"Saving one dog won't change the world but surely, the world will change for that one dog"

Except, it's not an accurate statement at all. Saving one dog most certainly changes the world. Saving one dog changes everything. Partly that's because of our relationship with dogs. Dogs have evolved alongside of humans since practically the dawn of time. We have developed a symbiotic relationship with them that we don't share with any other animal on the planet. They are family members, coworkers, team members, caretakers and confidantes. We develop deep and meaningful relationships with them; relying on them to comfort us, protect us, love us and help us in a hundred different ways. Their importance in our lives cannot be undervalued.

Did you know that it was the love of his dogs that helped Charles Darwin formulate his world-changing theory of evolution? Did you know that it was the loss of a special dog that led famed anthropologist Jane Goodall to Africa to study chimpanzees? During a visit to the University of Redlands in 2011, Ms. Goodall said:

"I learned everything I know about animals in general from the dog I had as a child. He taught me that animals have personalities and minds and feelings and what a true friend was. I never would have been able to go to Africa if Rusty hadn't died, because I would never have been able to leave him."

But these are just famous examples. Take a look at it from the simplest, most common standpoint. Imagine for a moment that you advocate for a dog on death row in a shelter and then that dog gets rescued because of your actions. Three things are immediately changed: you, the dog, and the people who have him now.

You are changed because saving the dog has made you feel good. You feel empowered, and most importantly – you *believe* you can make a difference. You advocate another dog, and another. Each dog that is saved because of your actions gives you more confidence. You realize that it's possible to affect change wherever you apply yourself. Who knows what the long-term effects of that will be? Maybe that empowerment will motivate you to take your advocacy to the streets; to foster a shelter dog, to volunteer as a rescue transporter, or to volunteer at a shelter. Maybe you will expand your efforts beyond animal advocacy and feed the hungry, or clothe the homeless, or fight for human rights. Whatever you do affects others, who undergo their own internal and external changes, who are able to make different choices and attain different goals because you helped them.

And what about that dog you saved? There is nothing more joyous and grateful than a dog that has been saved. Dogs don't keep those sorts of feelings to themselves, they want to share them. That dog becomes the most loving, faithful companion you can imagine. He will protect his new family in times of danger and comfort them in times of sadness. He will teach the children in the family to love and respect animals. Maybe knowing him will inspire a child to grow up to be a vet, or a zoologist. The dog will bring hours of laughter and joy to his people. He will keep them healthier in body, mind and spirit.

But there are even more possibilities. The dog you advocated for may become a service dog, helping a handicapped person live a less stressful life. Or maybe he'll become a therapy dog, and bring comfort and joy to the sick and lonely in nursing homes and hospitals, or help children learn to read in library programs. Maybe he'll become a search and rescue dog and save lives. There's just no way of knowing until he is saved. And you saved him, remember?

It didn't take money or power; it only took your hands, your head, and your heart. While no one person can do everything, every person can do something. A landslide begins with a single pebble set into motion. You are more powerful than you think. The world is changed.

The Stig

The gray pit bull with the white blaze on his nose had run out of time. He had been at the City of Cleveland Kennel for a week, more time than most pit bulls are afforded in city and county animal control shelters, and he was scheduled to be euthanized the next day. With less than 24 hours to spare, a worker at the kennel posted the dog's photo to Chris Hughes's Facebook page. Hughes runs the 501(c)3 not-for-profit Rowdy to the Rescue and agreed to take the dog.

Hughes named the dog "The Stig" after a mysterious character in the television show, "Top Gear" because nobody knew anything about the stray. Hughes evaluated him, determining that the dog needed basic obedience training. It soon became clear that The Stig didn't have an aggressive bone in his body, and would be a perfect candidate for Hughes's "Thera-Pits" program.

The Stig was trained at Elite K911 in Cleveland and received his certification to be a registered therapy dog. Once a stray dog living on borrowed time in a kill shelter, he now helps elementary school children learn to read in reading therapy programs throughout Northeast Ohio. The Stig also has the distinction of being the second pit bull to be accepted into the therapy program at Cleveland's Rainbow Babies and Children's Hospital, where he visits and comforts critically ill children.

Chapter <u>Two</u>
Becoming a Web Warrior

ANIMAL ADVOCACY AND RESCUE have changed dramatically over recent years because the Internet has become such a valuable and effective tool in saving lives. No matter what your time constraints; whether you have thirty seconds or twelve hours a day to devote to advocacy, you can become a Web Warrior. There are many different ways to advocate, from one-click advocacy to letter writing campaigns. This chapter will show you the fastest and simplest way to get started. Later chapters will guide you into more involved methods where advocacy begins to border on activism. You can save lives without ever leaving your house or your chair.

We live in a culture where everything moves at warp speed. We send instant messages via email, we order movies on demand, we carry cellphones so we are always in contact, we download books instantly, we get breaking news and information from the Internet, and we shop online. We expect everything to happen instantly.

It's fortunate, then, that there are existing websites where advocacy is just as instantaneous. You just need to know where to find them.

Freekibble

Freekibble [http://www.freekibble.com/] is a website that donates food to shelter animals. The site was launched in 2008, by the then eleven-year-old, Mimi Ausland. Mimi knew that there were tens of thousands of dogs and cats in animal shelters across the country, all needing a good meal. Freekibble was created with the goal to feed them. Today, the Freekibble Network reaches over 500,000 pet lovers who have helped feed over 8 million meals to homeless dogs and cats in shelters, rescues and food banks across the country. Freekibble has partnered with Halo Purely for Pets foods to accomplish this task.

On Freekibble's home page you'll find the Bow Wow Trivia game. Right or wrong, every day you click on an answer, Freekibble and Halo will provide kibble to animal shelters. There is a list of animal shelters currently in their program at: [http://www.freekibble .com/projects.asp].

TIP: at the bottom right corner of the webpage you can sign up for daily email reminders.

The advertising partners on the Freekibble website fund the food donations.

The Animal Rescue Site

Another good place to start your advocacy journey is by including The Animal Rescue Site [http://www.theanimalrescuesite.com] as part of your daily Internet routine. There are a number of places on the site where you can advocate. The home page has a big purple button that says "Click here to give, it's FREE!" When you click on that button, the site sponsors will donate food and care to animals living in shelters and sanctuaries. It takes less than two seconds to click that button, and you are already advocating!

> **TIP:** on the page menu to the left, select "Get Click Reminders"- you can sign up for a daily email to remind you to click.

Here's how it works: When you click on the purple button, your click is counted by the site's servers. Every click on the button results in funding for the site's charitable partners who care for rescued animals. The more people who click, the more bowls of food are funded.

The amount paid for each click is based on the advertising agreement the site sponsors have with The Animal Rescue Site. You can click once a day, every day of the year. Only one click per person is counted daily; there are filters set up to weed out multiple clicks. The more visitors who click each day, the more money is collected to fund the animals – so be sure to ask your friends to click too!

How it changes the world: Between 3 and 4 million pets are killed in U.S. shelters each and every year. There are multiple reasons for this tragic number of deaths; and funding care is one of them. Helping a shelter financially care for their animals helps to save lives.

From The Animal Rescue site: *"Bowls of food are paid for by The Animal Rescue Site's sponsors and distributed by The Fund for Animals, shelters supported by Petfinder Foundation, Rescue Bank, North Shore Animal League America, and other worthy animal charities supported by GreaterGood.org.*

100% of sponsor advertising fees goes to our charitable partners.

Since its launch in July of 2002, the site has established itself as a clear leader in online activism and a dynamic force in the effort to give all animals the happy, healthy lives they deserve. In The Animal Rescue Site's first year of operation, over 10 million bowls of food were funded for animals in need."

> **TIP:** If you don't want to sign up for daily reminders, you can set the site's home page as your browser homepage, so every time you launch your browser, you begin your Internet experience on The Animal Rescue Site.

Feeding shelter pets isn't the only way to advocate on the site. On the right side of the page, there is a column of icons. One of the icons says "Shelter Challenge." The Animal Rescue Site runs shelter challenges several times throughout the year, where you can vote to support your favorite animal shelter or rescue group. The organization(s) with the most votes during any given campaign are awarded grants of several thousand dollars. While a campaign is running, you can vote for your favorite shelter once every day.

    <u>**How it changes the world:**</u> Sometimes these grants are the one thing needed for a shelter to remain active.

Above the Shelter Challenge icon is the "Take Action" icon. A click there will take you to petitions sponsored by The Animal Rescue Site and its partners. The petitions cover a variety of topics and types of animals, and they frequently change as petitions reach their signature goals. Signing a petition is as simple as clicking and entering your email and name.

The Take Action Center will help you stay informed about current issues affecting wildlife and companion animals.

How it changes the world: Petitions cause changes to take place in animal welfare and in the laws protecting animals and prosecuting animal abusers.

The Animal Rescue Site isn't the only place online where you will find petitions. There are hundreds of active petitions advocating for animals on any given day.

Petition Sites

Online petitions empower people everywhere to make the change they want to see in the world. Petitions are used extensively in animal advocacy to change laws, prosecute people convicted of animal cruelty, remove animals from dangerous situations or neglectful caretakers, save animals from wrongful death and demand investigations. Search the words "animal advocacy" or "dogs" on the most popular petition sites: Change.org [http://www.change.org]; Care2 The Petition Site [http://www.thepetitionsite.com]; Forcechange [http://forcechange.com]; We The People [http://petitions.whitehouse.gov] and you will be presented with a page full of worthy causes.

The first time you sign a petition on any of the sites, you are required to register your full contact information – that's how they make sure that signers are real people. The White House site even provides you with a password. After you register, your information will automatically appear any time you view a petition on any of the sites. Once you are registered, signing a petition is as easy as a single click.

After you sign a petition you will be presented with a thank you page where it will be suggested that you share the petition with your friends. Sharing is a powerful way to maximize your signature's impact.

How it changes the world: Petitions create buzz and let officials and policy makers know that the public wants change.

DID YOU KNOW there are ways to customize your everyday Internet experience so you are automatically raising money for your favorite animal shelter or rescue group? There are two sites that will work for your cause every single day. The one-time set-up on each website only takes a few minutes.

iGives

If you shop online, consider installing the iGives add-on in your browser. The iGives button makes animal advocacy free and automatic. It's easy to get started: just register your name and email on their site [http://www.igive.com], and select the rescue or shelter that you'd like to benefit. If you don't find your favorite group in the list of those registered with iGives, you can add it.

When you download the iGive Button, it will automatically install on your browser tool bar. Clicking on the add-on will drop down a menu where you can view a list of over 1,000 participating stores, including Barnes and Noble, Amazon.com, JCPenney, Macy's, Staples, and more. When you navigate to a store via the iGives add-on and shop, a percentage of what you spend is donated to your cause or charity, at no cost to you.

iGive has donated to over 50,000 causes and charities since 1997.

> **TIP:** when you add a shelter or rescue group to the iGives site, have their address, phone number, and email contact handy.

Goodsearch

Everybody uses a search engine to find their favorite content on the Internet, so why not use Goodsearch instead of Yahoo, Google, or Bing? Like iGives, all you have to do is sign up on the Goodsearch site [http://www.goodsearch.com/], and designate the charity of your choice. From then on, as long as you are signed in to the Goodsearch site, every time you search the Internet using their site you automatically raise money for your cause – again, at no cost to you.

Unlike The Animal Rescue Site and Freekibble, every time you search using the Goodsearch engine counts – even if you search 100 times a day.

How it changes the world: The more money that a rescue or shelter has to operate, the more lives they can save.

C.a.WULFF

Chapter <u>Three</u>
Social Media is Your Friend

PERHAPS NOTHING ELSE HAS changed the face of animal advocacy and rescue as much as social media sites. Facebook and Twitter are the giants in this category with arguably the most powerful reach. Animal advocates and rescuers have latched onto these two sites and found unparalleled potential for networking animals all across the country – and in some cases, the world. They have developed a vast network of like-minded people who share information and skills to improve the plight of companion animals, effectively revolutionizing rescue.

Via social networking, breed rescue groups and specialty rescue groups are now made aware of dogs in need no matter where that animal is located in the country and can work together to improve the dog's chances of finding a home. There are even volunteers who transport rescue animals via car, truck, or plane to sanctuaries and adopters across the country.

Facebook

Facebook [https://www.facebook.com/] is presently the largest social network in existence. According to the statistics the company released in September of 2012, they had more than one billion active users. Of those, 526 million were described as daily users. If Facebook were a country, it would be the third largest country in the world by population. The number of daily users exceeds the entire population of the United States.

A social network operates by creating a domino effect. With customizable privacy settings, a person can reach whatever size audience they choose. An animal advocate who sets their privacy to 'friends of friends' will reach not only the people they are connected to but also all of the friends those people are connected to. The reach can be staggering.

If you decide to advocate for animals via Facebook, there are several things to take into consideration. If the majority of your connections are not people who are animal lovers or advocates, your update posts will not be reaching a helpful or receptive audience. Additionally, you run the risk of alienating friends and family by posting content that they are neither interested in, nor emotionally prepared to see. The last thing you want is for your connections to shut off your updates. This is the reason why many animal advocates on Facebook post only a few advocacy photos per day, or create a "crossposting" account. To be an effective advocate you need to have a network of connections who want to see and share your advocacy posts.

The most important thing is to build a reputable network. Try searching the word "crosspost" in the Facebook search bar. Each of the results are people who are advocating for animals. Some of the results will be community pages, and others will be individuals. This is a good place to start building your advocacy network by sending a few friend requests. Once those people respond, message them and ask them to suggest friends for you. Having an established advocate's recommendation will help you build a network of reputable people.

TIP: building a personal network is easier than building a community page following. Once you have an established personal network, getting your contacts to join your community page will be a breeze.

There are groups on Facebook for every type of animal advocacy imaginable. For dog advocacy, you will want to make sure that your network includes shelters, rescue groups, breed specific rescues, lost & found communities, groups that focus on senior and special needs animals, trainers, veterinarians and transporters. Each of these types of advocates may come into play at any time, depending on an animal's specific needs. An easy way to find rescue groups with a Facebook presence is to search the Animal Rescue Facebook Directory. [http://www.lacroixtees.com/fb_directory/ animal-rescue/].

How it changes the world: Raises awareness and educates others. Creates a community of cooperation with people all working toward the common good.

TIP: Remember – there are frauds and thieves all over the Internet, including among animal advocates on Facebook. Groups often raise funds for veterinary care and shelter "pull fees" using Chip-Ins. Always research a group before you donate.

Facebook Apps

Many Facebook users play games and use tools on the social network. These games and tools are called "Apps", which is short for "Applications." You may already be familiar with some of the more popular Facebook Apps like *Farmville* or *Words With Friends,* but did you know that there are also apps geared for animal advocacy?

A very successful tool on Facebook has been the **Pet Pardons App** [https://apps.facebook.com/petpardons]. It allows users to get involved in trying to save dogs & cats on death row in shelters and pounds across the country, in addition to promoting pets in no-kill shelters. The two main ways that users can get involved is by advocating and posting.

Anyone can post a pet to the Pet Pardons app. It's just a matter of gathering basic information about the pet you want to list. You'll need the pet's name, age, breed, identification number, shelter/rescue location, euthanasia date (if it's a kill shelter) and photo. The pet you post will be automatically listed in Pet Pardons so others can advocate for her.

Advocating for a pet via the Pet Pardons app couldn't be easier. Under each pet's photo is an "Advocate" button, and all you have to do is click it. The app automatically posts a photo of the pet on your Facebook page along with all of the animal's information so your contacts can see it and share it. The more people who advocate and share each dog & cat, the better the chances of the pet being seen by someone who can rescue or adopt—thus, granting the pet a "pardon."

You have the option of entering your email address when you advocate so you can be updated if the dog is saved. Since the app's launch in December of 2012, it has helped to save tens of thousands of animals.

The animals listed in the Pet Pardons app can be searched by breed, location, or pet name. Using the app is free. Pet Pardons is not a 501(c)3, does not generate an income and does not benefit in any way (financially or otherwise) from the listing of any pet. Pet Pardons is privately funded by anonymous donors. The Pet Pardons app is currently being developed for iPhone.

Pet Pardons also has a community Facebook page where calls to action are often posted.

How it changes the world: Brings awareness to the plight of animals in kill shelters, provides new opportunities and saves lives.

If you enjoy playing games like Farmville, you might want to try out the Facebook app **Joy Kingdom** [https://apps.facebook.com/joy kingdom]. Created by Sojo Studios, an American company specializing in the creation of socially conscious gaming, Joy Kingdom is part game, and part charity drive. The app is designed to raise money for a variety of good causes.

Sojo Studios in conjunction with The Animal Rescue Site and their sponsors fund food for animals in U.S. and Canadian shelters when you play five days in a row. You can also choose to "give joy" in-game to one of several animal welfare projects or community outreach. The more "joy" you give to a project the more money goes towards it in the real world. The projects are brought to Sojo by the Humane Society of the United States, the World Wildlife Fund, Best Friends Animal Society and others.

Sojo partners only with reputable not-for-profit organizations registered as 501(c)3 eligible. They maintain a transparent relationship with players and give progress reports and updates in-game.

How it changes the world: Helps to pay for pet food and vet care in underprivileged communities, promoting responsible pet ownership.

Twitter

Twitter [https://twitter.com/] has about one-fifth of the number of active users that Facebook has, but linking the two networks can be another valuable tool for advocating. Twitter is a fast way to share humane issues in the news and to drive people to your Facebook page.

Twitter is a real-time information network meant to connect you to the latest stories, trends and news that you find interesting. Users communicate using quick, frequent messages called "Tweets". Each tweet is a maximum of 140 characters long, demanding concise language to convey your message.

You can follow any person or organization on Twitter without sending a friend request. As you begin to follow rescue groups, bloggers, and other animal advocates they will often follow you in return. The network lends itself to cause and action. You will find links embedded in tweets to petitions, news stories and photos. A plea for help or a call to action can spread like wildfire on Twitter.

The # symbol, called a "hashtag," is used to indicate keywords or topics within a Tweet. Hashtagged words that are popular or used often can become a trending topic. Using a specific hashtag can be a good way to get users to follow an event or cause.

How it changes the world: Can rally sup-porters to causes by educating and informing.

Dogster

Founded in 2004, before the immense popularity of Facebook, Dogster [http://www.dogster.com] was the first social network for dog-centric people. The site has an estimated 750,000 members and requires users to create profile pages for their dogs and when communicating with other members, to use their dog's personas. This bit of roleplaying creates a friendly and polite community.

Dogster is a great resource for all types of dog related information. There are private groups and public forums ranging from dog health to entertainment. The forums of interest to dog advocates are: Rescue, Adoption & Happy Endings; Dogster Railroad; and Dog Laws and Legislation.

The Rescue, Adoption & Happy Endings forum is for dogs needing new homes and for sharing stories of dogs who have found homes through Dogster or through the love and efforts of rescuers. It is also the place to discuss shelters, rescue organizations, rescue strategies, issues, and solutions. Dogster also has a Dog Adoption Center [http://www.dogster.com/dog-adoption/]

powered by Petfinder (see chapter four). Shelters and rescues may create a shelter account and post their adoptable dogs in the adoption center. Individuals can share adoptable dogs by creating Dogster profile pages for them and posting about them in the proper forum.

TIP: If you are trying to find a foster or adoptive home for a dog, try setting up a profile page for that dog and post your plea in the proper forum. Don't forget to check the "adoptable" box when you set up the dog's member page.

The Dogster Railroad forum is a place to arrange for community transport of rescues or dogs being rehomed. It has become commonplace in rescue to transport animals across state lines from full shelters to those that have space; from rescues to foster and adoptive homes; and from shelters to breed specific rescue groups and sanctuaries. Transport coordinators map out a route and ask for volunteers to drive each leg of the journey. This forum is a place to ask for help in arranging a transport.

The Dog Laws and Legislation forum is for discussing legislation and legal matters pertaining to the rights and welfare of dogs. You will sometimes find action alerts in this forum as well as discussions on a multitude of dog welfare issues and ordinances.

How it changes the world: Encourages meaningful discussion and fosters a cooperative atmosphere.

Bella

In January of 2011, Examiner.com ran an article about Karlie Smick, an amazing nine-year-old animal advocate from Ohio. A month later, Karlie's mother, Kelly, contacted the reporter about an email she had received regarding a dog

in Akron. The email was from a college student named Traci.

Traci lived in an apartment next door to a man who kept a cocker spaniel chained to a dog house in his yard. The student was concerned because although the dog was being fed, she had poor shelter from the weather, and seemed to be in pretty bad shape. Mostly blind and mostly deaf, the little Cocker didn't even have a name. Any time Traci stopped to give the dog a little attention, the man tried to give her the dog. Unable to take the dog herself, Traci was hoping she could find a rescue to step up.

The Cleveland Pets Examiner contacted Dogs Deserve Better; a rescue group devoted to saving chained and neglected dogs, via Facebook. The organization put the Examiner in touch with their Akron representative Krysta Sue. Less than a week later, the man surrendered the dog to Krysta, who named her "Bella."

Bella had been a stray that had ended up chained in the man's Akron yard after he had accidentally hit her with his car. She had been on the chain for almost a year. She was matted and dirty and needed vet care. Pleas were posted on Facebook asking for help. Alyssa of

Dog Days grooming in Bath donated her services, and Annie, a business owner in Stow donated the funds to vet her. The vet estimated Bella's age at about ten.

DDB and the Cleveland Pets Examiner both advertised the need for a foster home for Bella via rescue groups and dog advocates on Facebook. Perla at Angel's Rest Animal Sanctuary in New

Richmond, Ohio agreed to take Bella. Angel's Rest is a non-profit sanctuary that takes in special needs pets, giving them the love and care they need for the rest of their days.

The next step was to obtain transport for the Cocker from Akron to New Richmond, a distance of about 280 miles.

Kathy Smola, an OTRA Verified Transport Coordinator in Cleveland, posted the information to her group of drivers and within hours, several volunteers had signed on to transport Bella the next day. (Smola can be found on Facebook as "Smola's Rescue Railroad.")

Krysta drove Bella to Wooster where she met up with transporter Jody. Jody drove Bella to Mansfield to meet up with Maddie and her husband Edd, who run *The K-9 Koach Rescue Transport van*. They drove Bella to their home  in Columbus, where they kept her overnight. The following morning, Maddie and Edd met up with

Debbie from Cincinnati, who drove Bella from Columbus to New Richmond, and handed the sweet girl over to Angel's Rest.

While at Angel's Rest Sanctuary, Bella received further medical care, then, was fostered until she was adopted into a forever home with a family who loves her.

C.a.WULFF

Chapter <u>Four</u>
Dogs in Danger

ONCE YOU BEGIN ADVOCATING on social media websites, you will find that there are groups advocating for all types of dogs in need. There will be animals on death row in shelters, there will be animals with serious injuries and medical conditions in rescue, there will be senior pets, abandoned pets, owner-surrendered pets, dogs rescued from dog fighting rings, lost pets, and groups devoted to specific breed rescue. All of them are pets in some kind of danger.

You will have to determine for yourself which need speaks to you the most. Whatever your focus, you will find that all of these types of dogs at one time or another can be found in shelters, and since more than four million pets are put to death in U.S. shelters every year, you may want to concentrate on helping stem that tide.

Although a no-kill movement began gaining momentum in 2009, wholesale change doesn't happen overnight, and thousands of shelters will still be euthanizing animals for years to come. Trying to make a difference can feel a little bit like swimming in quicksand, but you must remember that *every life saved makes a difference.*

Every time you share an animal that someone has posted on social networking sites, you help make those pets in need visible to more people. But you may be wondering by now how they find those animals to begin with. A good place to look is on websites where shelters list the animals they have for adoption.

Petfinder

The Petfinder website [http://www.petfinder.com/] is a central place where 13,969 U.S. shelters and rescues list the animals they have available. You can search the Petfinder site by shelter name; by location, and by breed. Once you have received search results, you can refine the search by pet's age, gender, size, and more.

There are all manner of shelters, and some are worse than others. Some have kill rates as high as 99%. Some shelters automatically kill certain breeds. Some kill inhumanely by gassing, or heartsticking, or worse. Some have reputations for killing even though there is plenty of shelter space, and others have reputations of cruel and inhumane treatment.

Unfortunately, not all of the most horrible shelters are listed on Petfinder, but some are:

- Miami Dade Animal Services, Miami FL
- Memphis Animal Shelter, Memphis TN
- Robeson County Animal Shelter, St. Pauls, NC
- LA County Animal Care & Control, Baldwin Park, CA
- City of Houston BARC Animal Shelter & Adoptions, Houston, TX
- Hernando County Animal Services, Brooksville, FL
- Humane Society of Goodhue County, Red Wing, Minnesota
- Vance County Animal Shelter, Henderson, NC

To advocate for animals in these shelters, find them by beginning a search on the Petfinder home page. Mouse over "Shelters & Rescues" in the purple bar, then, select "Find an Animal Shelter or Rescue Group."

When you find the shelter you are looking for and click on the name, you will navigate to that shelter's Petfinder page. The shelter pages always have a link to click so you can view the animals they have available for adoption.

> **TIP:** the Petfinder search engine is not very reliable when searching by shelter name. You'll have better luck searching by city and state, then looking for the shelter in the search results.

When you view an animal you will find links to share that pet on various social networks.

Although some of the worst shelters do not have Petfinder pages, there are rescue groups who devote their energies to saving the animals in them via their own Petfinder pages, Facebook pages or websites. These are some of those groups and the shelters they concentrate on:

Save the Devore Dogs
[https://www.facebook.com/SaveTheDevoreDogs]
Working to save the animals from the Devore
Animal Shelter in San Bernardino, California.
Devore is one of the most notorious shelters in the
U.S.

Stop the Slaughter at NYC ACC
[https://www.facebook.com/StopTheSlaughterAt
NYCACC?ref=ts&fref=ts]
Working to save the animals at the New York
Center for Animal Care & Control in Manhattan
and Brooklyn.

NCHS – Newnan Coweta Humane Society
[http://www.petfinder.com/shelters/GA207.html]
Working to save the animals at Coweta Animal
Control in Newnan, Georgia.

Friends of the Animals,
Troy, Montgomery County, NC
[https://www.facebook.com/pages/Friends-of-the-
Animals-Troy-Montgomery-County-
NC/284082615046247?ref=ts&fref=ts]
Working to save the animals from Montgomery
County Animal Shelter in Troy, North Carolina – a
facility that is reported to have a 99% kill rate.

Gaston County NC:
Available Pets in Animal Control
[https://www.facebook.com/GastonACNCavailabl
epets?ref=ts&fref=ts Gaston] Working to save the
pets at Gaston County Animal Control in Dallas
North Carolina.

Furever Friends of Fairfield County Dog Shelter
[https://www.facebook.com/FureverFriendsOfFCDS?ref=ts&fref=ts]
Working to save the dogs at Fairfield County Dog Shelter in Lancaster, Ohio.

ARNI Foundation
[http://www.arnianimalrescue.org/foundation/]
Saving the dogs of Putnam County Pound in Palatka, Florida.

Humane Society of NE Florida
[http://hsnefl.org/]
Saving the dogs of Putnam County Pound in Palatka, Florida.

Craigslist
Shelter animals aren't the only pets in danger. While the Internet has revolutionized advocacy and rescue, it has also created websites and situations that pose terrible dangers to pets. One of those sites is the immensely popular Craigslist [http://www.craigslist.org].

Craigslist is an international community for posting free advertisements. Users advertise all sorts of items on the site, but unfortunately, it has become a thorn in the side of animal advocates. Users are not permitted to sell pets on the site.

From the Prohibited Items FAQ on the Craigslist website: *Household pets of any kind including dogs, cats, primates, cage birds, rodents, reptiles, amphibians, fish. Re-homing with small adoption fee OK. Pet animal parts, blood, or fluids are also not permitted, including stud/breeding service.*

Although Craigslist prohibits the sale of pets on its network, that restriction has not stopped people from posting pets free, which places those pets in terrible, sometimes fatal danger.

Pet owners who offer their family pets "free to a good home" aren't usually bad people. They are often desperate people going through a major life change who feel unable to care for their pet any longer. They are almost always ignorant of what can happen to a pet offered "free."

1. People tend to value what they pay for. Pets obtained for free are less likely to be spayed or neutered (or vetted at all) by their new

owners and <u>more</u> likely to be abused and/or discarded.

2. There's a big market in selling pets to laboratories that perform experiments on animals. "Bunchers" gather free pets until they have enough for a trip to a Class B Dealer who is licensed by the USDA to sell animals from "random sources" for research. Random sources include strays, stolen pets, seized shelter animals, animals purchased at flea markets–and pets found through "Free to good home" ads. Bunchers will sell the free animals they obtain for $25. apiece to Class B. Dealers.

3. Free animals are taken to "blood" dogs in dog fighting operations — to train them how to kill, and to enjoy it. This can be dogs and cats, of any size. Often, a larger dog's muzzle will be duct-taped shut so that he can't bite back, and the fighting dog will gain confidence in killing a dog larger than he is.

4. Sometimes free puppies or kittens are "adopted" by owners of large snakes, who feed the baby animals to their reptile.

5. Unaltered purebred dogs offered "free to a good home" are often "adopted" by puppy mill owners, who use the animals for "breeding stock".

Although Craigslist prohibits the sale of pets, they do allow users to ask for a "re-homing fee."

It's an advocate's job to be a voice for animals, who cannot speak for themselves. You can help the animals in danger on Craigslist two different ways. One option is to "flag" any post that offers a pet free and Craigslist will remove it. Although that solves the short term problem, it doesn't solve the long term problem. Flagging a post often angers the advertiser and won't stop him from creating a new ad, either on Craigslist or some other site.

The second option is to educate the person who is offering the free pet by replying to their advertisement with educational material explaining the dangers and how they can change their ad to keep their pet safe. Several sample form letters are included in the back of this book that you can copy and use for this purpose. If the animal advertised is a pure bred, you can append the letter to suggest a breed rescue group.

TIP: not everyone likes to be shown the error of their ways, so you may receive an unfriendly reply. Don't let it bother you or goad you into an email war. Try to be content that you have made an effort.

Miss Elizabeth Bennet

Although John Varga is paralyzed on one side, he walked the Tow Path in the Cuyahoga Valley National Park every day with his small dog, Kinsey Millhone. When Kinsey was diagnosed with kidney disease and not given much time, John's wife, Kathleen, put the word out to a rescue friend that she was looking for a larger dog. Kathleen worried that Kinsey would not be well enough to walk with John, and she worried about his safety.

Kathleen's friend, Ellen, Facebooked her a photo of a terrified eight-month-old yellow lab mix that was scheduled to be euthanized the next day. The dog was at the Mahoning County Pound and had become very popular with volunteer staff there. Kathleen told Ellen she'd take her.

The director of the pound, concerned that the dog might mistakenly be killed in the morning, kept the dog in his office overnight to prevent any mistakes. The next day she was spayed, checked for heartworm and vaccinated.

Close to Home Animal Rescue transported the dog to the Vargas. They named her Miss Elizabeth Bennet. Kinsey is still with the Vargas, and Lizzie has become a great addition to the family, playing with the couple's other dog, George Bailey, in the big fenced backyard of their farm.

C.a.WULFF

Chapter <u>Five</u>
The Power of Words

I T HAS BEEN SAID that a picture is worth a thousand words – and it's true that many photos shared on the Internet can grab instant attention and go viral. However, there is also a time and a place where words are an effective tool.

Petitions

Chapter two showed you how you can instantly advocate for animals by signing petitions found at online petition websites. But the time may come when you are not able to find an existing petition for a story or cause that has moved you. Fortunately, anyone, anywhere can start a petition and win campaigns for social change. A petition can immediately mobilize hundreds of people locally or hundreds of thousands around the world, to make governments and companies more responsive and accountable.

When the Internet was just beginning to gain popularity, people were creating petitions and circulating them via email. These attempts were not successful because it was impossible to track the number of signatures. A petition will only work if it is able to accrue valid signatures and if those signatures reach a policy maker.

Three of the most popular petition websites: Change.org [http:// www.change.org]; Care2 The Petition Site [http://www.the petitionsite.com]; and We The People [http://petitions.whitehouse.gov] all work the same way. When you create a petition on any of the websites, you are required to name the person or organization you are petitioning. Each signature a petition receives automatically sends an email to the person or organization who has been named. Hopefully, as hundreds, then thousands of emails come pouring in, the person is motivated to make the change requested.

It may sound overly simplified, but it really works.

If you decide to create your own petition there are tools on each site to help you get started. The most successful petitions have certain elements in common.

- The goal is compelling and achievable.
- The petition signatures are delivered directly to the decision maker.
- Social media websites are used to spread the word and recruit supporters.

TIP: give your petition a short, descriptive, and urgent title, like: "Stop the Gassing at Fairfield County Shelter." Try to keep the title to less than ten words.

Do a little research to determine who the target should be. You might want to designate the president; a senator, congressman, local official or other policy maker; or the CEO of a corporation.

TIP: choose an effective target – someone who can really make things happen.

Write your petition in simple, articulate, convincing language so the goal is clear and the reason to sign is evident. Tell people right from the outset why they should support your petition. Make it easy for them to understand what you are trying to do. Shorter petitions with bulleted points or paragraph breaks are more successful. Be passionate, but don't leave out the facts!

If you are using the We The People Website, you have just thirty days to get 25,000 signatures in order to get a response from the White House. Additionally, it's up to you to get 150 signatures so your petition will be publicly searchable on the website. You need to share and promote your petition in all the most effective places online; social media sites, interest groups, any place animal lovers gather.

TIP: Grow your support base: Get your story to the media; start a social media conversation; ask people to share; organize a call-in day.

The websites have guides online to help you promote your petition and gather supporters.

Letter Campaigns

Almost every media outlet and elected official these days has an email address, making letter campaigns easy to organize and carry out from your computer keypad. Writing letters can increase awareness of your cause and help apply steady pressure to create change.

Elected officials are supposed to work for the people they represent, but unless you tell them what you want them to do, they very often do nothing. A letter writing campaign is a method of making your voice heard and of asking officials and decision-makers to take a specific action.

Letter writing campaigns can also be designed to reach media outlets in order to publicize a cause and gain supporters. Well-timed and clearly written letters can effect political decisions, especially in local government. Many elected officials keep track of constituents' support for issues, because although there are fewer people who write letters than vote, those who write are recognized as being more *likely* to vote.

As you begin to organize a letter campaign, be sure that you are totally informed with the facts of the issue, including background information. Write a sample letter or two that others can copy and make personal changes to, and make them publicly available. Make sure you know who the letters should be reaching; know which official or decision-maker has the authority to make the change you are asking for – it's a waste of time and effort to appeal to officials who do not have the authority to help you. Finally, get the information to the public. Post about your campaign on social networking sites, set up a Facebook event page and invite people to join, and ask your email contacts to participate.

TIP: if you are trying to make change at the state or federal level, direct potential letter writers to websites that will make it simple for them to reach their representatives such as [http://www.senate.gov/index.htm] You'll be surprised how many people do not know who their elected officials are.

If you are writing a Member of Congress, remember that the congressperson is not likely to actually see your letter. They have staffers who handle correspondence. Constituent services are high on their list of priorities, so be sure to inform them you are a registered voter. Since many issues come to the floor for debate or votes each day, a congressperson's staff will help them track the issues and constituents' support.

The work of creating and changing laws takes place in committees and subcommittees. If you are trying to influence an issue at that level, you will need to write to the committee chair. That person will seldom be your own representative.

Keep letters brief and to the point. Be factual and ask for specific action. Create volume; a large number of letters will illustrate the level of concern.

Letters to the Editor
Research has shown that letters to the editor are among the most widely read features in a newspaper or magazine, so writing a letter to the editor can be a good way to get your message to a wide audience to educate others and try to influence them to take action. Letters from readers can generate community discussion and stimulate interest in a subject. A letter to the editor differs from a letter to Congressmen and other officials because it is meant to be a statement of personal opinion. You can use emotions, facts, or emotions and facts combined to express your opinion. In addition to being read by subscribers, your letter may still reach policymakers, who keep an eye on opinion pages to see what issues are important to the public.

Although editors don't publish every letter they receive, if your letter is well written they are more likely to pay attention to it even if they receive multiple letters about the same subject. Shorter letters have a better chance of being published – under 200 words is best, because newspapers and magazines have limited space. Short letters will also make you sound more confident. Make sure your most important points are mentioned in the first paragraph. Your letter may be edited and editors tend to do that from the bottom up. If your letter is in response to a letter by another reader or to an article, say so right away.

Create an opening for yourself by keeping an eye out for articles about pets, because you can use practically any pet story to springboard advocacy. If the newspaper writes about a local shelter, use that as an opportunity to write to the editor about the importance of spaying and neutering. If an article appears about a dog show, use that opportunity to tell people how they can adopt a purebred pet from a breed rescue. If there is an article about strays, remind readers to license and microchip their pets.

These days, publications prefer to receive letters from readers via email because everything that's published is set up on computer. When you visit a publication's website, there will usually be several ways listed to contact them and one of these should be a contact email for the editor.

Always include your name, address, email address and phone number in case the publication needs to contact you. If you don't want your full name to be published, state so clearly.

Blogging

If you are good at communicating via the written word, there is one place that can indisputably be the least restrictive for advocating: *your own blog*. There are many blogging websites to choose from, all offering similar features. It doesn't cost anything to get started, and the basic features are usually enough for anybody. Two of the most popular free blogging sites on the Internet are Wordpress [http://wordpress.com/] and Blogger [http://www.blogger.com/].

Both sites will offer ways for you to customize the look of your blog and will offer similar tools and plenty of space on their servers for you to get up on your soapbox and get your message out.

You won't need to know any website coding to make a blog using these sites, it's as simple as using a word processing program.

The name of your blog can be the difference between success and failure. Keep it simple. Choose a name that is easy to remember and understand. Remember that your blog is a reflection of you, and it is where you will tell the world what you know.

The hosting websites will ask you to describe your blog. Have a clear idea of what you want your blog to accomplish and who your audience is before you write a description. Web crawlers will pick up keywords for search engine results, so say what you mean.

Keep your content relevant, original, and simple. If you have a lot to say on a certain subject, consider breaking it up into two posts, and insert a little space between paragraphs. Huge blocks of text can be very hard on the eyes when reading on computer, and some readers won't bother.

Every blog website has default themes to help you design your soapbox and make it stand out. There is also usually an advanced setting where you can add your own customized banner, making your blog even more individualized. When choosing a "look" remember that simpler layouts with lots of white space are more inviting for readers.

TIP: stay away from using black or dark backgrounds.

Be selective with any widgets you add in the margins, as too many will just detract from your content.

If you want your blog to reach a significant audience, you'll have to think carefully about your content. Once you know what subject(s) you'll be concentrating on, determine what's already out there and make sure you are not just duplicating something that already exists. You've got to write something worth reading, worth sharing, and worth coming back for more.

Blogs are typically an informal forum, so write as though you are having a conversation with a friend. Give your readers something to take with them; whether it be a thought, a piece of trivia, or an image.

Take advantage of tags, or keywords. Search engines will use those keywords to find your blog. Search engines won't be able to determine what your post is about automatically, unless it is at least 300-500 words in length, so give them some help. Think about who might want to read about your subject and what words they might be entering into a search engine to find related content, and use those words and phrases as keywords.

Finally, submit your blog to the major search engines like Google, Yahoo, and Bing. Each search engine has a procedure, so look for their guidelines and follow the instructions carefully.

Puppy Killer

In 2011, an animal abuse case in West Virginia created such an uproar that multiple petitions were created asking for maximum sentencing of the accused.

The young man on trial had obtained 29 "Free" pets from classified ads which he had tortured, mutilated, and killed in order to terrorize his girlfriend.

Even though 22 of the 29 charges against him were dropped, The judge hearing the case sentenced the man to 10-45 years in prison, an unusually long sentence for animal abuse in any state. The prosecutor explained it was because there had been such a public outcry, and that the judge had received thousands of letters and petition emails from around the world.

Chapter Six
Fundraising

IT IS INEVITABLE THAT once you are enmeshed in animal advocacy, you will come across rescue groups whose efforts really touch your heart. Most 501(c)3 not-for-profit groups accept donations through their websites, but of course, in today's economy, you may not have any disposable income to donate to their cause. You may want to think about setting up a fundraiser for that special group. Fundraisers can be achieved completely online.

Always ask permission from a group before embarking on a fundraising project for them. If you are planning on using PayPal [http://paypal.com/] as the online service for collecting the monies, be sure to get a letter from the 501(c)3 organization you are raising fund for, saying that you have permission to do the fundraiser. PayPal has strict policies. As soon as they become aware that you are collecting money for a charity they will require a copy of the organizations tax-exempt status. Have it in advance and fax it and the permission letter over to PayPal before you begin your fundraiser. Without this information in hand, PayPal can lock your account and make the funds inaccessible for up to six months – or until you can provide the documentation they need.

TIP: the Internet is so rife with scammers that it's best to protect the group and yourself by being completely transparent about your fundraising effort and its outcome. That means that you'll have to keep records and be able to post them publicly at a moment's notice.

Online fundraising can be carried out in a variety of ways – and is limited only by your imagination. Auctions and raffles are two very effective methods and can be held on private websites or through giant public venues such as eBay and Facebook. Keep the mission of the group in mind when asking for donations of items to auction or raffle. You'll be surprised how many people and businesses will be happy to donate an item to a good cause.

TIP: hit the ground running! You can get your auction moving quicker if your donators are willing to ship their item directly to the winning bidder. All they will need to provide is a photo of the item for you to get your project underway.

Prepare a short letter to help you ask for donations. Describe the event you have planned and provide information about the group you are fundraising for, including a link to the group's website.

Think in terms of a theme. If you are having an auction, for example, make it an art auction and ask a number of artists to donate an original piece of work; or make it a book auction and ask various authors to donate signed copies of their books. If you are planning a raffle, ask animal-related businesses to donate items and certificates for free services and assemble them into themed raffle baskets.

TIP: Plan ahead! People budget from paycheck to paycheck, so be sure to have everything in place and start promoting your fundraiser a week or two in advance.

For raffles: pick and announce your raffle winner within 48 hours of the raffle's close.

For auctions: stay on top of bidders and donators to see that everybody follows through in a timely manner.

Provide your beneficiary group with detailed documentation when you release the funds to them.

Angel

Rosemarie LaPierre had wanted a Papillon for ages, even since she'd been a teen. She had just never been in a situation where having a dog was a good idea. That didn't stop Rosemarie from keeping an eye on Papillon adoption sites.

In November of 2012, Rosemarie saw a dog on the Papillon Haven Rescue website that really stuck with her. The dog's background was sketchy. She had been an owner surrender from a divorcing couple. The  dog showed some signs of neglect, her coat matted in a double layer from the base of her tail to her ears. The rescue also believed that the man might have kicked her, because she was foot shy and afraid around men.

Rosemarie contacted the rescue and filled out an adoption application. Because she is in Massachusetts and Papillon Haven is in Ohio, the rescue contacted their Massachusetts representative to do a home check to make sure Rosemarie and her home were good candidates for an adoption. Once Rosemarie was approved, networking kicked into high gear.

When the call went out that transport was needed from Ohio to Massachusetts, drivers started responding with how far each of them could take her. The route legs filled in as far as Philadelphia, but then they hit a snag. One of the rescuers contacted another transport service called Libertina, and again the emails started to fly. An entire second network formed for the trip from Philadelphia to Massachusetts. The final transport consisted of four drivers from Ohio to Philadelphia, an overnight stay, and eight drivers from Philly to Rosemarie's home. The entire process took about two weeks and a dozen drivers, but today, Angel is safe and cherished in her forever home.

Chapter <u>Seven</u>
Taking it to the Streets

YOU MAY FIND THAT animal advocacy is enough for you, or that it's the gateway to something more. For those who feel like they are just getting started, it may be time to take your advocacy to the streets. Of course, that means getting up out of your chair and taking some sort of action.

Fortunately, there are things you can do yourself, as well as lots of rescues and shelters who need volunteers if you have the time and the means to help them.

Education

The free pets on Craigslist aren't the only free pets in danger. Several times a year thousands of kittens and puppies find themselves in the same precarious position when people offer their unwanted litters free via yard signs and public bulletin boards. You can be the voice for these innocents by keeping some flyers with you in your car.

Drop a flyer about the dangers of offering free pets, and the reasons for spay and neuter, in the mailbox at houses where baby animals are being advertised, or swap a bulletin board advertisement for free animals with a flyer about spay & neuter.

In summer, carry flyers about the dangers of leaving pets in cars on hot days. If you come across a dog that's been left in a car, leave a flyer under the windshield wiper.

If you know of a dog that is chained outdoors all day every day, drop a flyer off about how keeping a dog tethered is a danger to both dogs and people, and accounts for the majority of dog bites in the United States every year.

You will find sample flyers in the back of this book.

Shelter Volunteers

Shelters and rescues that house animals are always in need of volunteers for various tasks. Dogs at a shelter spend day and night inside of cages. All dogs need exercise, and being constantly caged can trigger behavioral issues, making it even harder for a dog to find a forever home. Cages need cleaning and there isn't always enough shelter staff to do that, or to exercise the animals. Sometimes the only exercise a shelter dog gets is the walk that a volunteer gives them. The more the dogs socialize with human visitors, the more relaxed they will be when potential adopters come looking. If you have a few hours a week to spare, check with your local animal shelters about being a dog walker or helping clean kennels.

Fostering

Some rescues do not have a kennel to house animals and instead, rely on foster homes. A foster family welcomes a rescue animal into their home until the dog can be placed in a forever home. Foster homes are less stressful than a kennel environment. They give a dog a structured home life, keeping him stimulated and social, and allow the foster family to work with the animal to correct any behavioral issues. Additionally, every dog who is fostered from a kennel environment opens up a space for another dog to be housed.

A foster home is a valuable asset for both a dog and a rescue group. It allows the dog's temperament to be evaluated in a real-life situation, giving greater insight into whether there are any behavioral issues that need work. A foster home is where the rescue will find out how the dog behaves with different types of people and other animals.

If you foster a dog, you will see to the dog's daily care, provide some basic training and behavior modification, see that the dog gets medical care, and dole out loads of affection. Many rescue groups will cover the cost of feeding and vet care for a foster animal in your care.

The goal, of course, is to find a permanent home for the animal. While you are fostering, the rescue group will be actively looking for potential adopters. The time spent being fostered will help the dog be relaxed and acclimated to home life, and therefore be more likely to stay in an adopter's home permanently.

In most cases, fostering a dog is a short-term commitment, not a lifelong one, although it is a twenty-four-hour-a-day obligation.

If you are interested in providing a foster home, contact your local humane society, local rescue groups and animal shelters.

Rescue Groups

Rescue groups typically offer programs throughout the year for their animals and the community. The programs can range from adoption events to low-cost spay and neuter programs, feral cat initiatives, pet food drives, and more. Whatever they have on their agenda for the year, you can be sure that they will need volunteers to help them at the events.

Some of the tasks volunteers are usually needed for are:

- Answering phones
- Collecting donations from collection boxes
- Placing containers for pet food drives and collecting the donations
- Being a booth attendant at pet events
- Scheduling spaying and neutering
- Setting up tables and booths
- Creating signage for events
- Showing animals at adoption events

Transport

Another area of rescue that always needs volunteers is transportation. There are groups devoted solely to getting an animal from one place to another, even across the country. There are groups that transport using volunteer drivers and others that use volunteer pilots.

Transport is a detailed and exacting undertaking. A transport coordinator determines the best route for getting a dog from point A to point B, then, structures the trip into "legs". Each leg is a 1-3 hour drive. Then the coordinator fills the legs of the journey with volunteers from neighboring areas. For instance, a dog being transported from Texas to Wisconsin will need drivers in all of the states along the way. Drivers work on an exact schedule. Each driver takes the animal a designated distance where they meet up with the next driver and the animal, health certificate and other documentation transfers hands.

Volunteers register on networks where transports are in the planning stages. Dog transport volunteers usually donate their own vehicle, gas, and crates to drive a leg of the transport.

Some places to register as a transport volunteer online are:

Dog Rescue Railroad
[http://pets.groups.yahoo.com/group/Dog_Rescue_RailRoad/]
[http://dogrescuerailroad.org/]

AHeinz57 Pet Transport and Rescue
[http://www.aheinz57.com/transports.htm]

Dogster Railroad
[http://www.dogster.com/forums/Dogster_Railroad]
You may have to register on Dogster first.

 Pet Transport Net
[http://pets.groups.yahoo.com/group/PetTransportNe
t/]

All Breed Rescue
[http://groups.yahoo.com/group/allbreedrescue]

Dog Transport
[http://groups.yahoo.com/group/DogTransport]

There are many more, and also transport groups
for specific breeds. You can find extensive lists of
transports on the following websites:

A Furry Friend
[http://afurryfriend.wordpress.com/animal-
transport-services/]

Dogs in Danger
[http://www.dogsindanger.com/transport.jsp]

    Volunteering for transport can be a very rewarding experience. It is taking part in saving a dog from a kill shelter and getting the animal to safety. If you can donate just half a day once a month, you can be a transporter.

Bentley

Bentley, an Australian Shepherd mix was stuck at the Central Missouri Humane Society in Columbia, and things weren't looking good for him. He had been found in a field covered with fleas and ticks. He was six or seven years old, making him a senior. Senior dogs are often passed  over at shelters because of their age and his time at the shelter was running out. But Bentley's luck changed when the Humane Society took him to an adoption event at Petsmart in one last effort to save his life.

Elizabeth Kramer was working at the pet store as a dog trainer, and when Bentley turned on the charm with his huge brown eyes, she fell in love with him and adopted him on the spot. Elizabeth trained him in basic obedience, and Bentley learned quickly because he is very eager to please and very smart. The only thing Elizabeth wasn't able to break was Bentley's separation anxiety.

Because Elizabeth was in school and also working full time as a dog trainer, Bentley was spending a lot of time at home alone, and he was acting out by destroying her apartment. That's when her mom, Pam, stepped in and took him. Pam says that she had fallen in love with Bentley. He passed his Therapy Dogs International (TDI) certification with ease and goes to school with Pam where he is a therapy dog for children with emotional problems. He is so smart that when students are sitting in a circle, Pam can point to each one and Bentley will go up to that child for petting. Everyone loves him and knows him by name at school.

Chapter <u>Eight</u>
How to Report Abuse

REMEMBER, BEING AN ANIMAL advocate means being a voice for the voiceless. That includes keeping their well-being in mind and speaking up when necessary. Many times, people witness animal abuse or neglect and ignore it, feeling like it's none of their business, or that they shouldn't get involved with what someone does with their pet. *But reporting cases of animal cruelty is the right thing to do*, (and you can remain anonymous).

Animal cruelty is not only wrong—it is against the law. All U.S. states have animal cruelty laws, and 47 states treat some forms of abuse as felonies. The ASPCA reports that without phone calls from concerned citizens reporting cruelty in their neighborhoods, they wouldn't know about most instances of animal abuse, and animals would stay in dangerous and hurtful circumstances, unable to tell anyone, and unable to defend themselves. Animals are dependent upon concerned citizens who recognize the abuse to get them the help they need.

THE FIRST STEP is to *recognize* and *identify* cruelty. Remember, an animal doesn't have to be hit to be a cruelty case. Depriving an animal of food, water, adequate shelter or necessary medical care is *neglect*, which is a form of cruelty.

There are two categories of animal neglect: **simple neglect** and **gross, willful, cruel or malicious neglect**. Simple neglect is failure to provide basic needs, such as food, water, medical care and shelter. It is not always considered a criminal act, and can often be resolved by the intervention of local animal care and control or humane agencies. However, some states make a distinction between simply failing to take adequate care of animals and intentionally or knowingly withholding food, water and medical care. Accordingly, "willful" neglect is considered a more serious, often prosecutable offense.

When determining if the animal is neglected, consider the animal's physical condition. Does he have a flea and tick infestation, open wounds – or signs of multiple healed wounds, patches of missing hair or injuries causing limping? Does he appear too thin? Is his collar so tight that it has caused a neck wound or has it become embedded in the pet's neck? Is the animal horribly matted? Are nails overgrown? Does the animal have heavy discharge from the nose or eyes? Is the animal visibly confused or extra drowsy?

Does the animal have adequate shelter available? Is the area kept clean of feces? Are there food and water bowls? Are the bowls empty or turned upside down? If the bowls are empty check back several times over the next couple of days at different times of the day to see if the bowls remain empty or ever get re-filled.

In cases where you suspect neglect, talk to the animal's owner if you feel comfortable doing so. Remember that you always catch more flies with honey than with vinegar. Don't accuse, just get the facts. If an animal looks starved, you might find out it has just been rescued. If it has open sores, you might find out it is receiving medical attention. You might also find that the people lack the resources to provide the best care to their animal, and need financial assistance.

TIP: don't ever threaten to call law enforcement or the humane society when speaking to the animal's owner. Threats cause people to be defensive, which is counter-productive to helping an animal in danger. Instead, offer suggestions and solutions.

If you are witness to a person actively beating or torturing an animal, intervene! Step in to help the animal, as long as you feel safe doing so. Animal torture is illegal, so you have the right to stop it.

THE SECOND STEP is to document the abuse and neglect. Include dates, times and the nature of the problem, even if you just *suspect* abuse or neglect. Photographs and videotape are helpful, though not necessary.

Try to gather the following information before submitting a report of animal cruelty:

- A concise, written, factual statement of what you observed—giving dates and approximate times whenever possible—to provide to law enforcement.
- Photographs of the location, the animals in question and the surrounding area. But don't put yourself in danger! Never enter another person's property without permission, and be cautious around unfamiliar animals who may be frightened or in pain.
- If you can, provide law enforcement with the names and contact information of other

people who have firsthand information about the abusive situation.

THE THIRD STEP is to report the abuse to the proper authorities. Most cases of animal abuse or neglect can be reported to your local animal control. You will find their phone number in the government listing of your phone book. After you provide details, ask for the animal control officer's name and ask what action will be taken.

The police department that covers your city, town or county is required to investigate criminal complaints, including complaints of animal cruelty and animal fighting. *Animal torture or animal fighting should be reported to the police department*, as these are crimes. Call 911 if the fighting or torture is in progress. If you are reporting a dog fight, after you call your local police department, call the **dogfight hotline** at: (1-877-847-4787) You can receive an award up to $5,000 for information leading to the arrest and conviction of a dogfighter. All information is kept confidential. The line is answered 24/7. There may also be an animal control agency, society for the prevention of cruelty to animals (SPCA) or humane society that has authority to conduct investigations of cruelty.

To find contact information for your local shelter, check the yellow pages or visit the ASPCA's searchable shelter database [http://www.aspca.org/adoption/shelters/] of nearly 5,000 community SPCAs, humane societies and animal control organizations. To find out if there is an agency other than the police authorized to conduct cruelty investigations in your area, visit the ASPCA's state-by-state list of anti-cruelty investigatory-arrest powers [http://www.aspca.org/Fight-Animal-Cruelty/Advocacy-Center/state-animal-cruelty-laws].

Always keep a record of everyone you contact (official or otherwise), the dates of the contacts, and the content and outcome of your discussions. Never pass on a letter, photograph, or any documentation without first creating a copy for your file. Make it clear to authorities that you wish to pursue this case and are willing to lend your assistance if necessary, and **be sure to follow up**! If you stay involved, they're more likely to do the same.

Helpinganimals.com reports that persistence has saved countless animals from abusive people. If you are unable to get satisfaction from law-enforcement officers, they suggest you go straight to supervisors. If necessary, appeal to local government officials, such as the mayor, prosecutor, city council members, or county commissioners. A simple call to the media (TV and print) in your area can move mountains. News coverage often forces officials to act and can also scare the abuser into stopping the cruel behavior. News coverage may also inspire viewers who have seen similar acts to step forward and share their own accounts.

Please, get involved! Research shows that people who abuse animals are very likely to be violent to other people. If you see something, say something. Tell someone. Tell everyone. Post somewhere. Post everywhere. If one call to the authorities doesn't summon help quickly, 1000 calls will have a much better chance at it.

Additional resources

For concerns about animal cruelty in **pet stores** or about an **animal breeder**, contact the U.S. Department of Agriculture (USDA). You can contact its headquarters at (301) 734-7833, visit [http://www.aphis.usda.gov/], or send an email to **ace@aphis.usda.gov**. The USDA will direct you to the appropriate regional department to which you will be asked to submit your complaint in writing.

To report **websites** that display acts of cruelty to animals, you should first contact the website host or sponsor. Major providers of Internet service, such as AOL and Google, have Terms of Service agreements that restrict depiction of objectionable material.

The next step is to contact the Federal Bureau of Investigation (FBI) [http://www.fbi.gov/contact-us/field/field-offices] and the Department of Justice [http://www.justice.gov/contact-us.html] particularly if you are reporting "Crush" videos.

You can learn more about what's being done about online cruelty on the ASPCA website. [http://www.aspca.org/fight-animal-cruelty/online-cruelty]

Sample Letters

The following letters may be used in part or in their entirety, and may be changed to fit different circumstances.

Suggested for Craigslist "free pets" ads.
You can use this letter as a template or download it here:
[http://www.yelodoggie.com/Yourfreepet.pdf]

I saw your ad on craigslist for a free pet.

I'm sure you care about what happens to your pet and want to make sure that he/she gets a good home, but by offering your pet for free, in reality, you are putting your pet in very grave danger.

You may have heard that craigslist does not allow pets to be sold on their site, but they DO allow you to ask an adoption/rehoming fee. If you receive any responses about your free pet, would you please say that your ad is a mistake, and that there is a $25 adoption fee? (Any amount over $20 is all right, but please don't ask less than that.) The reason is because of the types of people who specifically look for "free pet" ads.

We'd all like to think that caring people who are dying to have a pet will answer a free pet ad, but the awful reality is that that is not the case. Here's what you can expect:

1. People tend to value what they pay for. Pets obtained for free are less likely to be spayed or neutered (or vetted at all) by their new owners and <u>more</u> likely to be abused and/or discarded.

2. There's a big market in selling pets to laboratories that perform experiments on animals. "Bunchers" gather free pets until they have enough for a trip to a Class B Dealer who is licensed by the USDA to sell animals from "random sources" for research. Random sources include strays, stolen pets, seized shelter animals, animals purchased at flea markets—and pets found through "Free to good home" ads. Bunchers will sell the free animals they obtain for $25. apiece to Class B. Dealers.

3. Free animals are taken to "blood" pit-bulls & other fighting dogs — to train them how to kill, and to enjoy it. This can be dogs and cats, of any size. Often, a larger dog's muzzle will be duct-taped shut so that he can't bite back, and the fighting dog will gain confidence in killing a dog larger than he is.

4. Sometimes free puppies or kittens or smaller animals are "adopted" by owners of large snakes, who feed the baby animals to their reptile.

5. Purebred dogs offered "free to a good home" are often "adopted" by puppy mill owners, who use the animals for "breeding stock".

    I know it seems crazy that this sort of thing goes on, but I see the evidence every day in animal rescue. There was even a story in the news in 2011 about a man in W.Virginia who obtained 30 pets from "free pet" ads and then he tortured and killed them to terrorize his girlfriend. [**http://tinyurl.com/84zymr2**]

Charge at least a $25 adoption free to discourage resale of pets to labs. (Some sources suggest charging no less than $100 for purebred dogs.)

Remember, the welfare of pets is in our hands. If you are thinking of surrendering your pet, please check out the alternatives at wonderpuppy.net to giving pets away, including tips on solving common behavior problems, moving, house breaking, new baby, allergies, pet health problems, and grooming tips. If there is no other alternative, this site lists things to consider in finding your pet a new home.

Suggested for Craigslist ads where pets aren't advertised "Free", but **there is also no mention of a rehoming fee.** You can use this letter as a template or download it here: [http://www. yelodoggie.com/Yourpetnofee.pdf]

I saw your ad on craigslist. Your ad doesn't mention a rehoming fee, but if you get any calls on this ad, please be sure to tell the caller that there is a rehoming fee of at least $25.

I'm sure you care about what happens to your pet and want to make sure that he/she gets a good home, but by offering your pet for free, you put your pet in very grave danger.

You may have heard that craigslist does not allow pets to be sold on their site, but they DO allow you to ask an adoption fee. The reason is because of the types of people who specifically look for "free pet" ads.

We'd all like to think that caring people who are dying to have a pet will answer a free pet ad, but the awful reality is that that is not the case. Here's what you can expect:

1. People tend to value what they pay for. Pets obtained for free are less likely to be spayed or neutered (or vetted at all) by their new owners

and more likely to be abused and/or discarded.

2. There's a big market in selling pets to laboratories that perform experiments on animals. "Bunchers" gather free pets until they have enough for a trip to a Class B Dealer who is licensed by the USDA to sell animals from "random sources" for research. Random sources include strays, stolen pets, seized shelter animals, animals purchased at flea markets–and pets found through "Free to good home" ads. Bunchers will sell the free animals they obtain for $25. apiece to Class B. Dealers. −

3. Free animals are taken to "blood" pit-bulls & other fighting dogs — to train them how to kill, and to enjoy it. This can be dogs and cats, of any size. Often, a larger dog's muzzle will be duct-taped shut so that he can't bite back, and the fighting dog will gain confidence in killing a dog larger than he is. -

4. Sometimes free puppies or kittens or smaller animals are "adopted" by owners of large snakes, who feed the baby animals to their reptile.

5. Purebred dogs offered "free to a good home" are often "adopted" by puppy mill owners, who use the animals for "breeding stock".

I know it seems crazy that this sort of thing goes on, but I see the evidence every day in animal rescue. There was even a story in the news in 2011 about a man in W.Virginia who obtained 30 pets from "free pet" ads and then he tortured and killed them to terrorize his girlfriend. [**http://tinyurl.com/84zymr2**]

Charge at least a $25 adoption free to discourage resale of pets to labs. (Some sources suggest charging no less than $100 for purebred dogs.)

Remember, the welfare of pets is in our hands. If you are thinking of surrendering your pet, please check out the alternatives at wonderpuppy.net to giving pets away, including tips on solving common behavior problems, moving, house breaking, new baby, allergies, pet health problems, and grooming tips. If there is no other alternative, this site lists things to consider in finding your pet a new home.

Suggested for Pit Bulls offered "Free" in Craigslist ads. You can use this letter as a template or download it here: [http://www.yelodoggie. com/Yourpetbully.pdf]

I saw your ad on craigslist. I'm sure you care about what happens to your pet and want to make sure that he/she gets a good home, but by offering your pet for free, you put your pet in very grave danger.

You may have heard that craigslist does not allow pets to be sold on their site, but they DO allow you to ask an adoption fee. The reason is because of the types of people who specifically look for "free pet" ads.

Pit bulls and other animals offered FREE area often "adopted" to **"blood" pit-bulls & other fighting dogs — to train them how to kill, and to enjoy it. Often, a larger dog's muzzle will be duct-taped shut so that he can't bite back, and the fighting dog will gain confidence in killing a dog larger than he is. -** *this is what YOUR pet is MOST in danger of.*

We'd all like to think that caring people who are dying to have a pet will answer a free pet ad, but the awful reality is that that is not the case. You should protect your pet's life by asking for at least a $25 rehoming fee.

Here's what you can expect from posting a pet free:

1. People tend to value what they pay for. Pets obtained for free are less likely to be spayed or neutered (or vetted at all) by their new owners and <u>more</u> likely to be abused and/or discarded.

2. There's a big market in selling pets to laboratories that perform experiments on animals. "Bunchers" gather free pets until they have enough for a trip to a Class B Dealer who is licensed by the USDA to sell animals from "random sources" for research. Random sources include strays, stolen pets, seized shelter animals, animals purchased at flea markets–and pets found through "Free to good home" ads. Bunchers will sell the free animals they obtain for $25. apiece to Class B. Dealers.

3. **Free animals are taken to "blood" pit-bulls & other fighting dogs — to train them how to kill, and to enjoy it. This can be dogs and cats, of any size. Often, a larger dog's muzzle will be duct-taped shut so that he can't bite back, and the fighting dog will gain confidence in killing a dog larger than he is. - *<u>this is what YOUR pet is MOST in danger of.</u>***

4. Sometimes free puppies or kittens or smaller animals are "adopted" by owners of large snakes, who feed the baby animals to their reptile.

5. Purebred dogs offered "free to a good home" are often "adopted" by puppy mill owners, who use the animals for "breeding stock".

I know it seems crazy that this sort of thing goes on, but I see the evidence every day in animal rescue. There was even a story in the news in 2011 about a man in W.Virginia who obtained 30 pets from "free pet" ads and then he tortured and killed them to terrorize his girlfriend. [**http://tinyurl.com/84zymr2**]

Charge at least a $25 adoption free to discourage resale of pets to labs. (Some sources suggest charging no less than $100 for purebred dogs.)

Remember, the welfare of pets is in our hands. If you are thinking of surrendering your pet, please check out the alternatives at wonderpuppy.net to giving pets away, including tips on solving common behavior problems, moving, house breaking, new baby, allergies, pet health problems, and grooming tips. If there is no other alternative, this site lists things to consider in finding your pet a new home.

Sample Flyers

You can create your own flyers or use the ones on the following page as templates.

For Spay & Neuter: The ASPCA also sells packs of 100 full color informative flyers on their website: [http://www.aspcaonlinestore.com/products/99301-why-spay-or-neuter-flyer-pack-of-100]

TIP: add a cute picture of a puppy or kitten to your homemade flyer to draw attention.

There are pre-made educational brochures recommended for distributing to owners of chained dogs.
Download a ready to print and fold brochure from the Dogs Deserve Better website:
[http://www.dogsdeservebetter.com/brochurepit.pdf]

Spay or Neuter Your Pet

Stopping pet overpopulation starts with you!

According to the Humane Society of the United States, approximately 3-4 million companion animals (cats and dogs) are killed in shelters every year. These are healthy, sweet pets who would have made great companions. You can help stem the tide of unnecessary deaths by spaying and neutering. Spay/neuter is the only permanent, 100 percent effective method of birth control for dogs and cats.

By spaying and neutering your pet, you can be an important part of the solution. Contact your veterinarian today and be sure to let your family and friends know that they should do the same. There are also programs in every community to help needy pet owners with the cost of this surgery. Check with your local humane society, SPCA, or rescue group to see what financial aid programs are available in your area.

A neutered pet ...
- **will be healthier**
- **will live longer**
- **will listen better and be easier to train**
- **will be calmer and more affectionate**
- **will be less likely to roam, run away, and fight with other animals**
- **will NOT produce kittens or puppies!**

Invest in your pet's future ...
it's a small price to pay for a lifetime of love.

Suggested for bulletin boards and distribution wherever free litters of animals are offered.

Free to a Good Home!
A Death Sentence.

This is how some people see your giveaway pet:
Free bait to train & blood fighting dogs.
Free snake food.
Free money from the research lab.
Free sacrifice for satanic rituals.
Free animal for malicious pranks.
Free animal to set on fire.
Free animal to insert a firecracker into.
Free to a good home to breed indiscriminately.

Now you know why rescue groups always charge adoption fees for their pets, and why they always screen so carefully for good homes. "Free" is all too often seen as "worthless" in the eye of the beholder.

Please, don't offer your pets FREE to a good home, it's like giving them a death sentence.

Volunteers who work endless hours to save pets from the horrors of abuse and homelessness bring this message to you. Permission to reproduce this flyer and distribute is granted, encouraged and greatly appreciated.

Glossary

ASPCA – The American Society for the Prevention of Cruelty to Animals. A humane organization working to rescue animals from abuse, pass humane laws and share resources with shelters nationwide.

Blog – Shortened from "web log." A Web site containing a writer's own experiences, observations, opinions, etc.

Buncher – A person who collects free animals and then sells them to Class "B" dealers, who in turn sell them to laboratories for experimentation.

Class "B" Dealer – Are licensed by the USDA to buy animals from "random sources." This refers to animals who were not purpose-bred or raised on the **dealers**' property. There are currently seven active **Class B dealers** in the U.S. who round up thousands of dogs and cats each year and sell them to research facilities.

Crush Videos – A type of fetish pornography in which young attractive women in high heels torture and eventually kill small animals by crushing or stepping on them. In December of 2010, President Obama signed the Animal Crush Video Prohibition Act of 2010 into law to re-criminalize the creation, sale, distribution, advertising, marketing and exchange of animal crush videos.

Gassing – A method of euthanizing shelter animals by placing them in an airtight chamber and pumping in carbon monoxide or carbon dioxide. Euthanizing any animal by means of a carbon monoxide or carbon dioxide gas chamber is inhumane to all animals, especially medium and large dogs, and is demoralizing to the shelter workers. Approximately 30 states still allow gassing.

Heartsticking – A method of euthanizing shelter animals by jabbing a poison-filled syringe through an animal's chest wall. The needle punctures layers of nerves on the way to the heart. If the syringe pulsates, it is in the heart. If not, the animal gets another sharp stab. Once in the heart, the plunger is pressed injecting "blue juice" (sodium pentobarbital) into the heart of the animal. Animals are supposed to be sedated and comatose before the procedure but evidence has shown that many shelters are performing heartsticking on unsedated animals, which is very painful and inhumane.

Transport – The practice, in rescue, of transporting animals from kill shelters to rescues, no matter the distance.

Cayr Ariel Wulff is an artist, author and animal advocate. She is a native Ohioan who has been involved in pet rescue for over twenty-five years. Wulff writes a pet column and animal books column for the online publication Examiner.com and authors the blog "Up on the Woof". Currently, she resides in a log cabin deep in one of the Nation's National Parks with her lifemate and five dogs. She attributes her love of animals to having been raised by Wulffs.

If you enjoyed this book, you can follow Wulff on the Internet via various websites.

The author's website: www.yelodoggie.com

Up on the Woof blog: thewoof.wordpress.com

Twitter feed: twitter.com/yelodoggie

Facebook page: C.A.Wulff

ALSO FROM BARKING PLANET PRODUCTIONS

The *Planet of the Dog* Series
by Robert McCarty and Stella Mustanoja McCarty.

Long ago there were no dogs on planet earth...
Invaders threatened Green Valley...children were kidnapped and taken to the Castle in the Mist...the King of the North kidnapped two of Santa's reindeer...the people on Earth needed help. These are the exhilarating stories of how dogs came down from the Planet of the Dogs® to teach people about love, loyalty, and courage – and to help bring peace to the land.

Planet of the Dogs **ISBN-13**: 978-0978692803
Castle in the Mist **ISBN-13**: 978-0978692810
Snow Valley Heroes **ISBN-13**: 978-0978692827

Available from amazon.com and other retailers

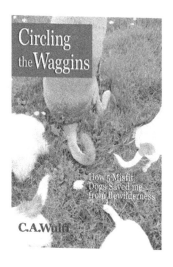

Circling the Waggins:
How 5 Misfit Dogs Saved Me from Bewilderness
by Cayr Ariel Wulff

More than twenty years of performing pet rescues could wear anyone down. Especially when the pets that end up being permanent residents in your home are the most irascible, insane and ridiculously un-adoptable pets known to man. Circling the Waggins follows two middle aged women as they maneuver through one unexpected pet debacle after another in a rugged and isolated cabin in the National Park.

ISBN-10: 0978692861
ISBN-13: 978-0978692865

Available from amazon.com and other retailers.

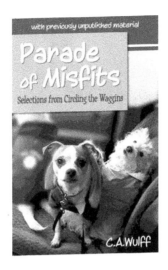

Parade of Misfits
Selections from Circling the Waggins

A mini-book of selections from the memoir "Circling the Waggins: How 5 Misfit Dogs Saved Me from Bewilderness." Includes the chapters "Lobster Tales" and "Joyful Noise" sharing what it's like to spend holidays with a pack of misfit dogs. Also included in this mini ebook are never before published essays about the author's dogs. Approx. 50 pages.
ASIN-B00B5LROQ6

Available in ebook only, from amazon.com.

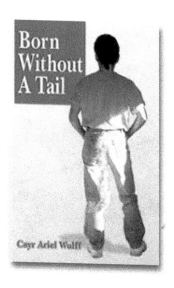

Also by Cayr Ariel Wulff
Born Without a Tail (2007, BookSurge)

When your home has a revolving door for abused and abandoned animals, keeping pets takes on a whole new dimension! Sometimes hilarious, sometimes heartbreaking, *Born Without a Tail* chronicles the true-life adventures of two animal rescuers living with an ever-changing house full of pets.

ISBN-10: 1419664360
ISBN-13: 978-1419664366

Available from amazon.com and other retailers.